LI

Fifty One Poems

Gerald Kells

LI

Poems copyright Gerald Kells, 2019

All rights reserved

Without limiting the rights under copyright reserved above, no part of this publication may be reproduced, stored in or introduced into a retrieval system or transmitted, in any form or by any means (electronic, mechanical, photocopying, recording or otherwise) without the prior written permission of the copyright owner of this book

ISBN 978-0-244-74534-9

'Orion in Winter' was first published in Diverse Verse 3 (Richard Archer) and 'Villain' in Poetry on Grey Squirrels (Fair Acre Press) 'Anthem for Dead Others' was commissioned by the Caldmore Community Garden for the Centenary of the 2018 Armistice. Particular thanks go to Richard Archer for his constant support and to the Walsall Poetry Society, Orators and Opinions and Yes We Cant for giving me the chance to read some of these poems in development.

Poems

I Advice from a Protestant Intellectual During the Irish Ascendancy
II After Storm Doris
III Almost Only White
IV Anthem for Dead Others
V At Old Dungeon Ghyll
VI Atonement
VII Autumn
VIII Before Noah
IX Book Protection
X Brer Rabbit and Brer Fox
XI Brotherswater
XII Bungalowland
XIII Caesar's Return
XIV California
XV Coming Down
XVI Counting the Days
XVII Crossing the Medway
XVIII Encounter with a Sheep near Buttermere

XIX Good Sense

XX Hellvelyn

XXI Hiroshige

XXII It's Rocks We'll Leave Behind

XXIII Lovers

XXIV Metamorphosis

XXV No

XXVI Oh Kindly Muse

XXVII On the Running of Hares

XVIII Orion in Winter

XXIX Painting Room

XXX Predator and Prey

XXXI Reassessment

XXXII Romeo and Juliet

XXXIII Safe Place

XXXIV Scale Force (1)

XXXV Scale Force (2)

XXXVI Sin

XXXVII Sitting Opposite

XXXVIII Snake Charmer

XXXIX Son House

XL Stiff Upper Lip

XLI The Carpenter of Nazareth
XLII The Client
XLIII The Oak Tree
XLIV The Parable of the Big Man and the Small
XLV There will be a day when I will be dead
XLVI The Rocks I Climbed
XLVII The Sorrows of a Hundred Centuries
XLVIII Trees
XLIX Tulip Tree
L Villain
LI What Makes This Sea Pool In

Advice from a Protestant Intellectual During the Irish Ascendancy

if you wish to describe the world
I would suggest 'The Principal Navigations'
by Richard Hackluyt as your starting point -
it's a collection of all things watery
done by Englishmen (and others) - there's
a plaque in Bristol Cathedral, calls him
a Harbinger of Empire, a Discryer
of New Lands, the man who found room
for his race - now dead, of course,
1545 or something, when only a few Negros
and other Spices crossed the Ocean,
before England grew richer, you Irish
poorer, the Catholic retreat, that perishing
of the World's Upstarts before
God's glorious (and relentless) advance

After Storm Doris

now that the ridge tiles have been taken away,
which came down in a rush once the first one went,
now roofers have been up with cat-ladders
and trowels and jacked-up replacements
on metal stanchions, brushed down the
driveways, now that a tree, which could not be
reset, has been sawn up into logs and
broom-ends, now there is no wind and no one
remembers that night when there seemed no
possibility the storm would desist or the
quiet continuation of life return or the
woman killed in Wolverhampton be forgotten,
now I re-enter the park and find it strewn with
shrivelled-round branches, like winter's excrement

Almost Only White

almost only white the snow
through which these moving branches show
what's out beyond their shadowed limbs,
a lip of garage, bent askew,
reflecting moon and silence too,
a night, like winter, holding breath
and cradling those enthralled to death,
who stare past this condensing rim
and seek a past they once set down
in memories which refuse to drown
but bob up from such depths below
as crack through ice and seal man's fate

a thaw will always come too late
as icy devils know

Anthem for Dead Others

they did not have to be white to die
or grow up in Oswestry with church nearby,
clutch pocket-book poetry as they stood in line
moustaches trimmed, revolver fine

they did not have to be white to die
on the pinching metal under pinching sky,
the girls who'd be hoping for better news
need not be in crinoline or tucked-in shoes

they did not have to be white to die
there was plenty of room when the Devil passed by
when it comes to destruction you will find
that mud and coffin remained colour blind

so remember in all your funeral songs
that Abram slew also his other sons

In response to Wilfred Owen's sonnet:
'The Parable of the Old Man and the Young'

At Old Dungeon Ghyll

here are the couple contemplating Bowfell
eyes into their Wainwright - dewy with anticipation

here are the couple - she's just done Jack's Rake -
thinks it the epitome of human achievement

here are the couple - Norwegian and English -
off on a shopping trip and Crinkle Crags tomorrow

each of these people discovering a landscape
inside the landscape that's outside this door

and here I am also, not sure what I'm seeing,
unable to see fully, since I'm lost without you

Atonement

when all the sins in the world have been committed
and each one graded and sorted into categories
and the tree of evil has been catalogued into species,
can be examined under a microscope, each fault
classified by its DNA profile - those genes of nastiness -
when we have understood the fundamental physics
of being cruel and merciless and manipulative
and all the broad definitions that we throw at others
not acknowledging them in ourselves, when all this is clear,
then our upright race can come to its conclusion,
its true reckoning, perhaps its redemption,
and your one act, still nailed there, still white-dead,
still bleeding, not atoning for every sin in the world
but for each one, or maybe for none of them,
will stand as confirmation to the Universe:
that the world's sins have all been committed

and order can be restored again

Autumn

if she falls to the ground when her body's still green
her eyes will shine out and her mind will stay keen,
if she falls to the ground when her body's turned yellow
her veins will pulse blue and her faculties mellow,
if she falls to the ground when her body's turned russet
you will see in her face that she's scared to discuss it,
if she falls to the ground when her body's turned brown
her limbs will have weakened, her thoughts flickered down,
if she falls to the ground when her body's turned red
you will tell from her eyes she intends to be dead,
but if she lingers in hope of a sprinkling of snow
she'll steal the space where new saplings should grow

every tree learns to shiver when frosty winds come
but the last leaf must fall before winter's begun

Before Noah

wherever you start you'll end up at the root of things -
from the most translucent leaf or dappled branch
through a similar fracturing of light and ligament -
even the bark of trees, if you look closely, twists
and corkscrews over sunless shadows, nooks and
boles of cancered wood, and, at the very base of things,
observe the foot of this monster, fat-arched over gaps
in which soil piles up by the same physical laws
which require a rise in the flesh between human digits,
a canvass-tautening over our grip on the world -
it makes me wonder why no one else but
Tolkien with his Ents or Wyndham with his Triffids
has let these things move, as move they must, when,
by the nature of the world, trees are one day given,
by both God and the Devil, the thing they currently lack,
the ability to escape destruction

rivers, on the other hand, and brooks and streams
can never stop still, they must be restlessly churning
downwards, whatever the incline or deceit, and,
as they wash past stone and slab, will curl up also
into waves which pulse with the reflections
of the sun, then chevron through narrows
between rock and rock, accelerating into humps
which flow elasticated over smoothed-down lips
that carry all before them, turn both the shallows clear
and the bedrock murky - how might a man examine
what physics operates beneath this top flow, pulling back

then edging into crevices which divide and scatter,
curving as a prism bends a spear to catch a soul
or, much more widely, a disapproving deity
will watch his people hack apart what's fixed and true
then bring down that which can't be washed away?

Book Protection

he spent the summer protecting his library,
using plastic liners you buy in rolls -
many of the books had come from his father's,
some were torn or mottled at the edges,
others had covers of tissue-thin paper
jacketed against the cold of a post-war freeze -
patiently he laid out these bomb-blasted fragments,
flat on their backsides, then, smoothing down the face,
cut back any extra before sliding into position,
peeling back the ribbon on the self-adhesive strip -
it's a knack and a fiddle, fitting back a dust-flap,
making sure its smooth enough to sit on the shelves -
he hoped he'd be finished before it got to winter
when the reading of books helps keep out the chill

Brer Rabbit and Brer Fox

so Brer Rabbit and Brer Fox sat on the porch
and told tales about cabbage patches and girls
and how they once tried to marry the same sweetheart
and Brer Rabbit could dance but Brer Fox could sing,
and Brer Rabbit said how he'd fix Brer Fox
to sing better so he'd get the girl because
Brer Rabbit hadn't a chance, and Brer Rabbit
told him to open his mouth but when
it was open proper, slit Brer Fox's tongue

so Brer Rabbit and Brer Fox met once again
and swung on their rockers and laughed at the past,
knowing that each had forgiven the other,
until Brer Fox invited his old friend inside
where the pot was steaming and the smoke snuck out -
later that evening I dropped in on Brer Fox,
who served peas and cornbread and a tasty meat stew,
danced like an angel with his neighbours all round him,
howled at the moonlight and sang like a bird:

'it is better to be living than boiled in a pot'

For Zora Neale Hurston

Brotherswater

from the crest between Angle Tarn and Place Fell
I look across to the fingered-out ridges over
Brotherswater and am reminded of the carved
claws of an Imperial Dragon set aside
for only the Emperor's vision -
                              how democratic now
that anyone can come up here and capture in an instant
overhanging clouds, bold strips of light, the almost mist-like
final hour before bliss is turned to absolute night

Brotherswater shines upwards, mirror to this passing,
its knees bent double among the more practiced fields -
they're green still as the fell-side is tanned by dying,
its gorse yellow, its ferns browned-over in obsequiousness

if the dragon breathes a little I do not notice,
it is too slow for the flicker of my camera-phone

we must get down from this saddle to our hotel room
where light and dreams will protect us until sunrise,
where strangers will gather for their evening meal,
not daring to twist the dragon or tempt the gods as
we have done on our long, out-twinning ramble from
Pooley Bridge, as Romans did, to Rampsgill Head
then down again to where all life must lead, an unlatched gate

Bungalowland

all the houses look like someone died in them,
the gardens made ready for the funeral cortege,
the blinds pulled across so the shadows hang heavy
on the winter light in stagnant rooms -

all the roads look like nobody uses them,
the pavements empty, the litter gone,
bins stand like pillar boxes, neat as sentries,
guarding the silence in-between homes

but look through the crannies from the surrounding fields,
people move like ants or thin, black spectres
following their trails from bed to bathroom
kitchen to sitting room, front door to grave

imagine the dullness, the mechanical dying
the once-more waking that has no purpose -
welcome to a world where no one is living
and all the houses look like someone's died.

Caesar's Return

when Caesar came back to Rome again
he brought Victory which all proclaimed,
he brought Empire and Plunder, Loot from afar,
the piling of Triumph on each of these stones -

when Caesar came back to Rome again
he brought Certainty, Euphoria, Mob Acclaim,
so many Defeated, so certain our Destiny,
a Pax Romana, never to be broken -

when Caesar came back to Rome again
his Legions of Corpses were not on our minds,
we'd Bowed out Heads, now they were Uplifted,
a Weighing of Sacrifice we agreed was in balance -

still we murdered Caesar
and our Adulation did him no good

California

in California they'll be planting oranges,
it's something to think about on a wet Sunday afternoon -
if the weather clears we can walk down to the broken pier
and watch the seagulls land beyond the keep-out sign -

it makes you think why all those dustbowl folks
traipsed out of deserts towards the sun,
makes all the newscast-reels and Guthrie songs
that whistle out of cinemas and crackly speakers

sound obvious - now, when I see a muddy shore
and questing sky beyond some one-arm bandit store,
I invent, if I'm honest under my plastic cape and cap,
that thing for which America's become a proxy:

a Californian vista in which oranges grow effortlessly,
where John Wayne leans on his saddle hard,
encompassing humanity, bright and true,
the freedom-lie that all believers stumble to

Coming Down

as if there weren't enough people on Slieve Donard
at five o'clock they were still piling up
in tattooed chests and red-raw elbows
with a bottle of water already three quarters drunk

children clinging to parents and Alsatian dogs,
a man who worried he wouldn't be down for the car park,
four boys playing on the ice house,
a girl in a brown bikini, nicely baked on a stone -

there'd been no one on the slopes up Slieve Commedagh,
the place as deserted as a Sunday afternoon in the rain -
you could imagine the Rapture in that beating sun
but why go to heaven when it clings to the cairn ahead?

you cannot chase away a descending line of hills
or catch them in a camera like fairy-fibs
but you can stare in wonder past Binnian to the sea
and imagine no troubles in this place, only sky forever

Counting the Days

they're talking about Revelation on the next table -
he brings up Beasts and Sacrifices and Lambs,
explains the intricacies of an exposition
that goes back to JN Darby and my teenage years -
he doesn't know who JN Darby is, nor does she,
yet out of ancient texts, out of antique words -
their meaning lost in the politics of Ancient Rome
and the persecution of a sect of fanatics
in catacombs and caves - he brings forth dreams,
prophecies of a world that's yet to come,
turned violent and wild, terrifying yet free -
his vision spins outwards like a Catherine Wheel,
demons cast down as new gods are drawn in -

I'm waiting for my blackbean soup
they're waiting for the end of days

Cafe Soya, Birmingham

Crossing the Medway

a man is working on the hulk of a submarine,
it is listing to one side and he has scaffolding
round its conning tower - in the silt-brazed strand
it could be a scuttle-brown tern or a
discarded engine boiler - it is neither kind
of jewel, just a hulk lying resonant, a tin-can
between Strood and Rochester - I think the Medway
is this right-angled waterway that curdles through
meandering grey, mesmerises like a thing blunted
or a corpse hemmed in with security fences and posts,
the clutter of railway infrastructure, two small boys
who stare into water and a house burnt out,
which is empty I suppose - once past this
fermentation I move into unassuming quiet

St Pancras to Faversham

Encounter with a Sheep near Buttermere

the mother, sensing her lamb was not there,
limped towards the other sheep, one and then
another who ignored her, chewing with
their bleak, black lambs - the missing lamb
had found its way, forwardly, into a
mélange of adults, kids, buggies and, once
there, ingested the attention of all
those maternal, cooing humans wanting
a camera shot with their newborn too

the mother, realising the situation,
bleated helplessly: I want my infant
back - but to no avail - what loss if older,
scruffier the lamb's rejected, dead? a
man must focus - kneeling on a sunshine path

Peggy's Bridge

Good Sense

the dissipation of all things said,
of all things broken, of all things read,
the passing outwards from between
of all things visioned, all things seen,
the execration of a single touch,
a chain-reaction of such and such
when what is smelt, as rank as days,
outspreads in poems, pacts and plays -

I taste this succoured verse anew
and each day sip the morning dew
which all my senses bring to one -
life will be ended as it was begun

come worms, whose virtue overtakes,
come, earthy and ribald in my wake

Hellvelyn

yesterday, after Hellvelyn, I had
the fells to myself, only the sun on
my back as I strode towards the path down -
my heart pounded up Dollywagon, the
thick end of a thousand feet of vertical
crumbling wall to an iron post
left by the Victorians in memory of
other climbers from Rydal to Sticks Pass -
twelve miles, a four-thousand foot climb
and Fairfield, still a haunt of flat, flinty stones

on the train today I'm among drunks and
stag dos and rugby fans that see me troubled and tired,
who snigger, like the mountain biker I caught
unhelmeted, full-dreadlocked, curt, who claimed
petulantly: 'I can go anywhere I like',
his words weighted by the world and Bacchus

the sun watched impassively as I ruined his day

Hiroshige

a tower like the core of an apple,
a bridge-arch covered in figurine dolls,
some trees, spindly-stalked, anorexic, clustered,
yellow homes, like lanterns in the landscape,
upturned with sliding screens, luminous guests,
the sea, blue-washed, ink-edged, flat-centred,
skiffs on the shore-line, unsailed boats lain in,
tarpaulins over their secret cargo-holds,
seven sails in the sea-ways, like sheets on sunken poles,
two, tooth-like, on the horizon turning
past the green distance of a hilly coastline,
down beneath the orange skyline, gripping
the edge of balance: ships, buildings, temples,
earth-gods, none straight or haphazard, these dark shapes

Demi Beach : Sumiyoshi : Sixty-One Provinces
(The Moon Reflected Exhibition at the Icon Gallery,
Birmingham)

It's Rocks We'll Leave Behind

it's rocks we'll leave behind not words,
those simple lichen-covered stones,
our complexities reduced,
like all the complexities of time,
to guess work in the fossil record -

time will level out Shakespeare and Milton
and newspapers wrapped round chips,
inspiration turn to dust,
while our monuments are sniffed round
by dingoes and tigers, by tiny rodents
who emerge from future crevices to
investigate the pools of our inheritance -

when future folk look down they'll stroke
these carvings, finger faces that invoke the dead

Lovers

so, Sir Lancelot, here's your Guinevere,
daggered betrayal in leaden eyes,
belonging to someone else, she's Arthur's,
spawn of Merlin's magical conceits -

try this fruit, it's lush for a moment,
its anger dredging out your weakest spot,
its bile silvery like dew on mountains -

so shall the great and godly prosper,
so shall the weak and worthless descend -

all that I listen for in silence is sleeping,
all that I hear in clamour is noise -

Arthur's the man who deserves the honour,
you, Sir Lancelot, overly beloved,
are prey to mistakes of valueless denial,

the motion of lovers now encased in a vial

Metamorphosis

in conclusion, in the end, at the last,
just when the pitiful and pitied and
the pitying's all past, then will we sing
psalms and songs and hymns and upraised lays
that Cooper, Faber, Watts and Wesley sought for
in their days - but how they failed in degree!

superlatives surrender to that day
as night to brightness every time gives way -

sound's majesty, sheer might and justice flee
as dreams before a dread reality,

and good with bad, with truth, with virtue rise
from vagaries to solid shapes, and hope -
such is its metamorphosis into light -
becomes a certain greeting of the eyes

No

there is a point when you have to say no,
it is exact, like pressing a pen in a wall -
if you decide the wallpaper's too nice
or the people who own it might complain
you will hesitate and your fingers falter,
the man who waits to dictate your obituary
will force a pen inside your fingers
and, instead of publishing convictions,
you'll write obsequiously, in text-book italics:

I am my brother's keeper, I do as he says,
he is my maker and my instructor,
by his laws I live my life out slowly,
bound to his commands, under God-like fealty -

beyond that point no one can say no

Oh Kindly Muse

oh kindly muse, upon the sons of men
your blessing pour, as in a previous age
Milton and Chaucer, Spencer and Shakespeare felt
your bleeding hand outstretched to those you choose,
that from the snow-bound heart may yet outflow
your warmth, a bud, a flower, a new-born spring,
a vast creation and a commodious world
for spirit to inhabit in its constant youth,
a world where such a creator is revealed
as sowed with stars the heavens thick as a field

breathe not as one presumptuous or devoid
of gratitude to him who rules the world
but mould the very substance of your work
into the open hands that God requires,
and, kindly muse, upon the sons of men
such beauty deal as truth may feel no pain

'And sowed with stars the heav'n thick as a field'
Milton: Paradise Lost, Book VII, l 358

On the Running of Hares

we're not setting any hares running,
we have no intention to alarm,
the public should be assured that
our plans are not specific enough
for their input at this time, for the moment
our aim is to establish a Strategic Case,
we'll release the hares when we know
you're safely in your beds, when they
can burrow under house and hearth
without disturbance, sap away
the strength from your foundations -
then, with all the evidence amassed,
we'll drop our bombshell,
how you should have objected earlier,
how you left it much too late

your house may be in ruins
but the hares will have moved on,
another project calls,
we do not want them knowing

Orion in Winter

looking out of the frosted window
he saw the moon and Orion cast their veil
across the slates of his neighbour's roof and
somehow, despite the cloud and the cold and
the fact that you could only see the belt
and one or two stars, he inferred comfort
from this stable constellation and its satellites:
nothing could go wrong with Orion in place,
steadily orbiting our planet, turning without pride

there, on his upstairs landing, he imagined the
world of Galileo and Copernicus had been
bypassed, that he was grounded again, at the
centre of his own Universe, on earth, rooted
unmovable, not worthy of his own discountenance

Painting Room

he started on the painting room today,
working through the easels and
pastels and bringing a cough to
his throat from dust-clouds and paper,
from bags and charcoal and hardboard
which he laid out over furniture
so the wrinkled-up lino and long-lost carpet
could reappear from the mess

a hardly-used electric typewriter
thrown in with the other junk
hems in a nearly-new computer
like some cyber-oasis in an old-style desert

his father would have been a hundred and one today
if his body of tissue and turpentine
hadn't been wrapped up in one last canvass,
its best-before-date pre-signed in a corner

Predator and Prey

so, in the night, the wolf came prowling
searching for prey in the moon's wan light -
how is the doe to escape this villain,
still and waiting for freeze-frame flight?

two eyes like wolf's eyes blink in the dark -
where is the silence in this midnight park?

so, in the night, the man sleeps sparsely
wakes in his bed with the scent of fear,
now he's alert to impending danger,
now the predator is drawing near -

is he the wolf when daylight returns
or is he the doe when night oil burns?

Reassessment

I bought a colander to sift my life,
it was orange and red and made of plastic,
I placed my life inside the colander
and sifted the contents as hard as I could,
a thin, grey dust fell into a sauce pan,
I stirred the mixture and added water,
I watched the dust spin into a pattern,
I stirred and stirred, looking for a message,
I ached so much I threw down the ladle,
I raged at the pan, upended its contents
which spilled on the floor, discolouring stone,
I sat in my armchair 'til the floor dried white,
then hoovered up the dust to throw in the bin -

I kept my receipt, I can still have my money back

Romeo and Juliet

staccato as a washboard from the deep south,
its bells flinching like a shaky tambourine,
searing as a long arm picking a guitar,
fretting like a mama screeching out the blues

sweet as a sugar cane sweating in Jamaica,
round as a water melon, slithery as a snake,
sensitive as the orange sun setting in the east,
or a cat devouring fowl-meat, gluttonous in its teeth,

green as a cotton-stem where the weevil never struts,
guttural as a chainsaw down among the pines,
wild as a buzzard or a juke-joint in swing
is my love and your love when the interval begins.

Safe Place

it has been a month since my mother died
and in that time I have hardly woken up,
I am still sluggish with the grief of it,
I know that there are things to do - tidying up -
and that there are other things - freedom things -
that I can do whenever I like - now she is gone -
but it's the starting out that turns more difficult
each time I try to expedite the future -

in the morning, after the alarm goes off,
there's a simple time when I can curl up
under my duvet, warm and undisturbed,
free of imperatives and obligation,
fear and opportunity -

if I wait five minutes the alarm will stay cold
like the vases I inherited on either end of the mantelpiece

Scale Force (1)

the path is rusted red from clodhoppers' boots,
the bridge is bolted through with rigid iron,
the side of the hill is laced with brown tracks
cut by children, running, yelling, caught short
when clambering the mountain ribs into
this cleft of tight-packed trees and dank rock,
a hidden-away place, a cathedral
high-vaulted under his holiness, the sky -

God's water, thin and righteous, falls so clear,
a singular shaft of white that hangs in space,
a kind of machine of wonder, a hidden
pool which gathers water at an altar-stone,
then tumbles strands of pearled opacity
on rocks that never should have been climbed

Scale Force (2)

it had rained two days before we returned,
there was a tree in the pool, its branches
splayed as if a wooden man had tumbled
and been twisted by the rocks, one long fall then
washed past a smaller waterfall down to
his final resting place behind a dark
assemblage of trees round a narrow slit,
shielded from winds and wiles of Lakeland storms,
misty and mardy, fickle and fright'ning -

long, thin wee of this crevice turns to flood,
the nearby fells have obviously been on the piss,
as if the night before a fight occurred,
some fir got in the way and was, by accident,
sacrificed to swaggering, drunken gods

Sin

given the wherewithal to sin, he said,
I'd sin as much as were agreeable,
while you, who do not care to take my part,
I would extinguish in a trice - once dead
would make your memory detestable
so those to whom you offer comfort howl:
our hero was not virtuous but foul

now, as you stand there in this vestibule
admiring marbled palisades ahead,
do you not see how luxury of heart
is made both easy and unstoppable?

first one forgets where sinning starts,
then bears deep hatred t'wards one's foes instead -

pure conscience shines less glorious in the dead

Sitting Opposite

the one speaks numbers into the tape,
the other points out engines he has missed
on sidings on the far side of the track,
and when we leave the shunting yard behind
into the scrub and saplings of our way
they play their tape, one sequence at a time,
some four, some five, some six flat-numbered nouns,
each represents an iron-besplattered train

the one is old as Cain after his sin,
the other hardly out of anoracked spots,
I move my husked belongings to a seat,
so I can concentrate my mind on this:
scrying out the jutting streets beyond
where such (and other dreamers) dare to meet

Snake-Charmer

music snake-charms at the back of the bus -
it makes a change from bhangra or hip-hop -
the notes entwine, like the fingers of a belly dancer -
so many people have got off on the way to Wolverhampton
that I stop reading, pick up pen and screwy paper and write
dreamy snake-charmer words which imagine
exotic transience, mint tea and bright hookahs,
a kind of civilisation that is dusty with age,
the passing of traders on a silk road to Nirvana,
turbans, dust-shawls and eyes nerved by sandstorms -
I wave at a camel-train passing fissured Willenhall,
its tarmacked frontages and newly built town houses
rain-spoilt and aching for some uncropped sun

Son House

when Son House plays 'Death Letter Blues'
and barks across the studio
it's time to stop, it's time to choose,
there's nothing else to do

he hits the strings so harsh it pains,
his voice is grainy, subtle too,
cradled in poverty, untaught retains
a peril that comes crashing through -

when Son House plays 'Death Letter Blues'
go fuck those pseuds in blue suede shoes!

Stiff Upper Lip

the Edwardians knew how to trim a moustache:
their first act to take scissors across the lip,
slice in one go through the overhanging mass,
then, when the most was done, seek flushed-up strands
and, with close-aiming, cut the buggers down

top and back require selective clipping,
being the business end where plans are made:

sever the trench towards the hill, Young Jim,
use your tickling comb to smooth the ground -
sniper the last survivors on that ridge

after the war flappers went smooth-faced
and only Hitler hacked at either side

moustaches now are rare as kites,
precision razors slice them down in seconds -
each time I go to shop they've grown a blade

just ghosts-on-ladders boast of whiskers worn:
ay lad, the proudest topiaries are easiest shorn

The Carpenter of Nazareth

there is also always the man who makes the coffins
in his annexed side-room, sound-proofed so only
an occasional hiss of saw-blade sizing in, or squeak
of virgin screws in key-drilled pine, leaks down the passageway
to those who wait on single chairs and in too much company

what does he look like, this chippy-man? how does he frown
over the execution of plane and sander? has he wrinkles
beneath the work-dust of his task, which is, if anything,
proof of our civilisation, that we don't leave bodies by the road
for the next slavering carnivore to scavenge on, its tongue put
                                                                                   out
as this man puts his own tongue out, slips a palm over field-flat,
ice-flat, street-flat, micro-flat surfaces, imagines moon-travel
where tolerances are burnt so minuscule they chart both
                                                                      advancement
and vulnerability, this search for nick and bruise, an
                                                               expressionless doctor
who repeats his sympathy from the other side of a table-top,
                                                                    softly saying:
'it's all gone for this one too - the universe ahead's no more than
                                                                        rooms
for waiting in'? some sap comes in to sympathise (p'rhaps he's
God's assistant) while down the corridor silence jars on metal -

the unseen coffin man has dropped a plaque on saw-dust floor,
startled us into noticing the granite headstones sat beside us,
marbled urns and signs - don't touch, they are not fixed in yet -
curtains, caught on an open window, frame the light outside,
an occasional breeze forces dust from other side-rooms in

The Client

she smiles as she visits him,
he's not ill enough for the grave yet -

she laughs at his witticisms,
his gallows humour which she's heard before,

and the things she hasn't heard before,
the places he's been, his mother and how he misses her,

someone who wronged him many years ago
and it was never made right but they've gone now -

she likes him in the way she likes all her clients,
not too closely that she can't walk away -

it's not what he wants, he wants
to be out there doing, climbing ladders,

walking hills, writing poetry that
will be remembered after he's gone - unlike this one -

there, she says, that's better,
leaves his dressing for the washing up -

it's all still there, where it shouldn't be,
heaped on a white-clean drainer

The Oak Tree

they're pulling down the Oak Tree in Friary Park,
so thick its cross section is taller than a man -
for years it's been half eaten away, the bark
gone crisp and termited on one side,
the last remaining branches out of balance,
wood tacked back like some deformity of
arson or lightning, the face of an old schoolteacher
or the burnt hide of Leviathan -
                                    logs lie scattered
over turf while two minuscule traffic cones
sit poxily tethering tape across a path -

we too are leaving, clearing out our house-bits,
filling up the garage, bins, a deep-holed skip -

fifty years seems paltry against this Oak's old age,
what's gone as fleeting as the next incumbent's trash

The Parable of the Big Man and the Small

I thought I saw David the other day,
you know the one who killed Goliath,
he's become a recluse, could have been a king
they say, if it hadn't eaten into him -.
they say he sees the slingshot in slow motion,
that he wakes up sweating and it's flying
off into the face of Goliath - we should
be glad, you know, I mean without David
we'd be living in Gath under Philistine
rule, but instead we're free to come and
go, it's just David who's imprisoned,
towered over by Goliath even when he's dead -
and that apartment he's living in, in Jericho,
it would kill a man, even a hero like David,
but you can see him, if you like, go to any
corner, he'll pester you with his begging

There will be a day when I will be dead

there will be a day when I will be dead
when other people will go about their business
and in their shopping bags and suitcases
and overflowing rucksacks and boxes full of tat
carry their lives through streets and alleys
and up to rooms and down to cellars
and pretend and lie and chat about nothing
and wait for buses and fan their eyes
in overheated, deathly cars -

dinosaurs will still be gone
hope still wear its trousers long,
I'll be dead and out of sight,
the world will not turn out the light

The Rocks I Climbed

I found the place I climbed the rocks,
source of my first nightmare -
someone moved it to Bloody Bridge,
I was sure it was in Newcastle -
I suppose it's how you formulate the words
and sentences that changes your perspective,
just as the sea, smashing into a harbour,
grinds down pebbles outside its crook
while inside fishing boats stay limpid
and fishermen stay wise

up above us Slieve Donard,
like some beached whale
in this reddened light, promises better
hides the rougher peaks behind -
someone curved in Binnian and Bearnagh
like flags in the wind with granite tips -
all ways round there's fuchsia growing wild
in pavement gaps and cliff-top ledges,
covering up derelict properties
between a rash of cheap bungalows

that nightmare passed but left its after image
like some photo cracked and faded with age -
I still feel the fear of it, crashing down the hill,
out under the bridge at Newcastle,
washing up dead, which is absurd
because it was the wrong bloody river

if anyone cared which river it was -
certainly not me, looking for a childhood
that has grown smaller as I've grown older
and further away as I've drawn near

The Sorrows of a Hundred Centuries

to dissolve the sorrows of a hundred centuries
would take more than wine, me-thinks,
for he who drinks merely abates those sorrows
until he is sober again

yet here we are again dissolving sorrow
with wine which flows unhindered from the vineyard
because we know no other way to temper fortune
which sober waits on our unsteady feet

alas, there is no better way of living,
even if this seems unlikely to the foolish,
for without wine a single moment
recalls those hundred centuries of pain

(however much we, each one, drink
we must return to sorrow again)

*Reply to the last line of 'Bring in the Wine' by Li Bai,
translated by Vikram Seth in 'Three Chinese Poets'*

Trees

who waits where the crevice turns
beyond the picture's edge, before these
silent pines, as close as blinds? can you
split the saffroned snow, the snowbells
prickling through the darkened mound? will you
leave the curling birch, and let the
frozen river duck you down into
pine-cones drifting, bark smoothed round?

who waits where the crevice turns?
what child-like witch or feral clown?

it is enough to stop for a moment and shelter,
strip the slush from your watery feet -
there is a path somewhere, you had it lately
but now don't know which way to turn...

what's half-conceived and half-believed
still just enough to halt your moving forwards

Trees, N Wall, 1937, Walsall Art Gallery

Tulip Tree

in Palfrey Park there is a Tulip Tree
which finally felt strong enough to flower this month -
in Canada it would be no surprise,
in fact a pip-squeak - they grow tall as ashes -
but here its tender yellow marks a change
and sets us browsing in our nature books -

they planted more but most were vandalised,
an act that left the few remaining shy,
nervous of crowds, of laughter, of the world -

as we were photographing there
a neighbour, Muslim and unknown to us,
commented on the fading light and how
we were so lucky to have a park like this -
yes, we agreed, and now the Tulip Tree has flowered

Villain

hunched over the latest discovery in his hoard,
spine arched so his tail curls round his back,
chunky as survival (unlike his pretty cousin)
examines the surface as a jeweller discovers flaws

unworried by surrounding foliage
(there are no predators that can challenge this thief,
no raptors or wolves, the cats are too small -
he doesn't need sanctuary to flee to in the night)

brazen, he isn't bothered by hatred or stones
which children throw to push him away
from bird tables or hedgehog trays
where feasts fall conveniently into his lap

no, he has treasure enough and more ahead
he is no rat-with-tail, this mountebank,
he is proud and will outlive us all,
even those little tykes who enjoy his persecution

What Makes This Sea Pool In

what makes this sea pool in
and in the still bay rumble over
itself, as rhythmic as the softening
beat of those who pass, hidden
by rock-crests and under trees
on stunted upper cliffs from which
silence out-plays and small birds
whistle and larger birds climb?

what holds this pooling in of turquoise
between deep maroon or, further out,
beyond the bit-ends of rock,
a stretching back to where the
waves start from a single, glimpsed line,
sketch-made, rubbed-clean,
uncharcoaled, always?

St Mary's Bay, Near Brixham

Endnote

Gerald Kells is poet and writer who lives in the West Midlands.

His poetry has been published in a number of magazines and collections.
He has performed his poetry at events all round the Midlands and helped organise a Poetry Reading to celebrate the People's Choice Exhibition at Walsall Art Gallery.

His novel, 'The Net Mender's Son', is also available as an e-book. His unpublished novel, 'The Floating Child', was long-listed in the Wowfactor Competition.

His short plays have been produced in London and the Midlands. His full length play, 'The E-mail History of Josef K', was long-listed for the Bruntwood Award.

He is a keen Fell-walker and Book lover.

THE NET MENDER'S SON
GERALD KELLS

Printed in Great Britain
by Amazon